Every poem has a story....and all my stories have a poem.
This is to everyone that inspired every verse.

Introduction

I'm damned..to live as the empty shell of a Man
Cursed to be a story that ends..before it even Began
I have limited time..so I try to do what I Can
To leave a legacy behind..so people can remember who I Am

But I'm Me...I'm not Sane
I see words dance around in my Brain
And every smile that I feign..keeps driving me more Insane
And I swear you can look...but no one else in the world is the Same

And this pen is attached by a chain to my Pain
To the words that keep haunting my brain..and the fear that runs through my Veins
For the ink will rain down on my page...and it bleeds and it Stains
Like the horror attached to my name...and again...I'm just me..I'm Insane

Look into My Eyes

I look into your Eyes
Yet you keep looking past Mine
With a heart as cold as Ice
And a blocked up Mind
Smile my way, as if that would Suffice
Open your eyes and quit being so Blind
...
Every time we Touch
These chills run down my Spine
You don't say Much
Still you look so Divine
Break out from this Hutch
I wanna make you Mine
...
Look into my Eyes
Give me no more Lies
Don't you Realize
That my heart still Cries
Tries to be strong even though it Dies
Don't Gaze up at the Skies
Just Look into my Eyes

Since You Left

You left Saying that I wont be Missed
My thoughts continues to come back to This
Replaying the last words I heard you Hiss
Taste buds still recall that cherry flavored Kiss
Estranged I'm stuck in this Abyss
Who else but you could ever make me feel Bliss
But its wrong of me to continue to Persists
I know..Somewhere.. someone who is right for me Exists
But.. until she is found.. of you I will continue to Reminisce

Never Forgotten

The story of my life...isn't written in a Book
It has no catchy song...with an impeccable Hook
But its been recorded in the memories..of the people that I've Met
And when I come to die, I hope, at least one person..wont Forget

And all I want...is for someone to remember who I Was
That when no one else remembers..at least I knows she Does
And everything that's died with me...will still be living there Inside
In her dreams...reliving every memory..that was spent right by my Side

And I don't care if History knows that I ever Existed
As long as you remember what it was to have me..and Miss It
I guess I'm just selfish..and want you to keep me close to your Heart
Even years after I'm gone...It'll be like we were never Apart

Remember the Old Days

Do you remember the old Days
When we would sit down for Hours
We couldn't find the right words to Say

That could express this love of Ours

We would just sit and Stare
Straight Into each other's Eyes
You could smell love in the Air
That..no one can ever Deny

But now you are far Gone
You went and left me Alone
You have a new place you Belong
A whole new life of your Own

A whole new world to Experience
A lot more love to be Found
Our love has no more Resilience
You no longer need me Around

Sometimes I stop to Reminisce
About that day in December
Yeah, the day of our first Kiss
I hope that you still Remember

Or do you at least Remember
The last kiss that we Shared
Drenched in the cold rain of November
I'll admit that that day I was Scared

Now you are far Gone
You went and left me Alone
You have a new place you Belong
A whole new life of your Own

A whole new world to Experience
A lot more love to be Found
Our love has no more Resilience
You no longer need me Around

Despite that I was Saddened
Despite all the tears I Shed
Despite all that Happened
Despite all my heart has Bled
Despite that now its Dead

I still want you to Know

That I'll love you Forever
And I'll never let you Go
I'll welcome you back Whenever
With a smile in my face..and a simple "hello"

But for now you are far Gone
And right now I'm Alone
You cry yourself till Dawn
Because you're all on your Own

The new life you Experienced
And the new love you couldn't Find
Turned to me for Convenience
Try to leave this new life Behind

We can talk about the old Days
Yeah we can sit down for Hours
I bet we still wont have the right words to Say
To express this love of Ours

Empty Shell

How will I ever Forget
The day that you walked Away
Tears left my cheeks feeling Wet
And my heart began to turn Gray
Though it still slowly Pulsates
It has now begun to Decay

How can no one Tell
I'm nothing but an Empty Shell
A body without a Soul
That no longer has self Control

But you still continue to live on like This
Pretending you're caught up in Bliss
But every time that you're with Him
Fool yourself to think its me you Kiss

To be a free bird

The reflection of my Eyes
Portray the bluest Skies
For my freedom is Disguised
Behind empty words and Lies
Inside this cage I'll Die
Waving the passing days Goodbye
For these wings will never Fly
Never soar up to the Sky

Without You

What the hell will I do
The day I can no longer have you
I'll be like a bird that never Flew
Or a sky deprived of Blue

You are the reason I live
And every smile I Give
Every breath that I take
The reason every morning I wake

The sky now begins to turn Gray
As my world begins to Decay
For now you walk Away
And my heart you begin to Betray

Even Atheist need relief

Sometimes we can't help but to fall down to the Sod
Wanting to scream our lungs out to this God
That deep down we know doesn't Exist
But sometimes pain blinds our judgment with a Mist
So we Pray up at the Sky
Hoping this God...Our prayers will Reply

Even though we know that he's not There
We still do it...every time the pain's too much to Bear

Cry yourself to Sleep

Well go ahead and cry yourself to Sleep
Shouting...and shouting my Name
Yeah, grab that knife and cut yourself so Deep
Come on slid open that Vein
And yeah..you can blame it all on Me
How I said you were nothing but a Game
But you knew thats how it was going to Be
And how your growing feelings were in Vain
So don't cling and cry words of Destiny
We both know it sounds so fucking Lame
So why don't you put yourself to Sleep
As you drown in your own Shame

A Peaceful Break up

You were my angel fallen from Above
Now we don't have any signs of Love
It's completely shattered into Pieces
Lost our hugs and passionate Kisses

Like our love, I wish that I was Dying
Your empty words are no longer Satisfying
You can tell me how you really tried your Best
Blame it on Me...yes..let it all off of your Chest

But don't kill me, just bury me Alive
And I promise ,death for me, will soon Arrive
I want these worms to feed off of my Eyes
And my body be completely filled with Flies

And When my eyes are completely hollowed Out
When my own existence..I begin to Doubt
Your essence should be wiped off of my Mind
Then we can both leave this empty life Behind

Every second Counts

Right now we are meant to be having the time of our lives
But time for me stopped the day you ran from my life
Maybe I forced it...that fight..a last strike..game over.. it's three outs
But I'm here begging for one more second..Because babe for me every second still counts

When will you be back? Im counting every second
We'll talk about our problems..together we'll dissect it
Our meeting must no longer feel like fate...maybe your love has turned to hate
But this heart stills yearns for you...so in me things have begun to complicate

Because babe I lost you...wasn't you that lost me
Don't you see...I lost us that dream house..we wanted by the sea
A house full of children..running and playfully screaming
Babe just wake me from this nightmare and tell me that I'm dreaming

Because that's exactly what this is...just a fucking nightmare
To wake up every morning and realize that you're not here
And the hardest part of this..was figuring everything out
A future that I lost for us....but babe...every second still counts

Dragging Dead Bodies
Watch it come up from your Shadow
Feel it staring at your Face
Feel your soul being taken down Below
As death holds you in its tight Embrace

Your life now runs through your eyes in Flashes
And your body seems to be breaking Down
So let your body crumble down in Ashes
And Be sure its your own blood in which you Drown

But theres no place for you to rest your Soul
For Heaven and Hell exist within us All
And even as you rot inside your Hole
Into the depths of darkness you shall Fall

Spiraling Down

I walk down this empty street at Night
Fighting the urge to shout out your Name
Like a moth with no wings, I can no longer Fly
I feel like I'm spiraling down towards a Flame

I walk towards a bride, climb on the Ledge
Then close my eyes and i hold My Breath
Thinking back to how you broke our Pledge
Open my eyes to find The Angel of Death

There it was...staring at my Face
Just floating there..with Its devilish Grace
My heart began to fasten its Pace
For this thing had no face just a skull in its place

There's no need to be Afraid
I'll make sure you feel no Pain
I know right now you feel Betrayed
I know it keeps driving you Insane

Just take this Step
And I'll free you of your sorrow and Grief
I promise you that Soon
I'll grant you sweet Relief

For what he promised I couldn't Wait
My heart was filled with rage and Hate
So I took a leap into My Fate
Hoping I'd reach Heaven's sacred Gate

On my Own

There is something that I have always Known
I'm meant to walk this empty world Alone
Even if you're beside me..I'm always on my Own
With dread, sorrow and loneliness..its the way I've Learned to Grow

So I'll throw away everything I've ever Owned
Embrace the dread that inside my brain has Grown
Just disregard everything I've ever Known
And leave all the fears inside my heart Alone

Watching the man inside the mirror becoming fully Grown
Letting reality unfold..the way I've always Known
It was my choice.. always being on my Own
Full of regret...I'm dying all Alone

Wake me Up

I am alive but I feel so Dead
Its getting hard to keep looking Ahead
With these eyes that are going Blind
And this brain that won't leave the past behind

Everyday it starts to Reminisce
Replaying in my head, every single Kiss
They keep on flashing in my head so Fast
Leaving me imprisoned in the Past

All my being feels like it's Asleep
Drowning in the darkness, already very Deep
Please don't let these wrist continue on to Bleed
Here, I'll admit it, You're the one I need

So give me a kiss and wake me Up
Make all these feeling burst and Erupt
With your breath bring me back to Life
And show me what its truly like to feel Alive

Please take away the Sadness
And Be my guarding Light
Guide me away from all this Darkness
And keep me safe throughout the Night

The last Words

So you decided it was time for you to Go
Leaving me speechless, I couldn't tell you all I wanted you to Know
Hoping there was a way for me to Show
All the feelings that in my heart, for you, still Grow

I stood in silence, watching you cross the door so Slow
Hiding in darkness, trying to keep my head down Low
Trying to hide the tears that for you began to Flow
And hoped you didn't see the puddle I created down Below

Out to the cold, you made your way throughout the Snow
Even in darkness, I could see your beauty shine and Glow
So I asked the question that my heart wanted to Know
"Will I ever see you Again?" of course, you just said "No"

Hopped in the car and called my name out, "Joe"
I looked up to see that her tears too began to Flow
"Its not what I want, but I really have to Go.
Never thought my feeling for you one day would cease to Grow"

And so She left, leaving marking on the Snow
Nothing but silence and the cawing of the Crows
I was finally alone, free to let my tears Flow
So I fell down to my knees and buried my face down on the Snow

Writing her Ballad

I wish there was more of me, to you, I could Give
But you're already the only reason, right now, I still Live
The only reason every morning i even try to wake Up
The reason I changed my views on how full the water's in this Cup

Still I don't understand how you became so important to Me
This heart that i locked..and you barge in without needing a Key
Just appeared in my life and took away the Depression
Making your way in my heart..becoming its newest Obsession

Never before had I needed someone So Much
My reason to Live....yet impossible to Touch
Years to wait before I can even hold your Hand
Counting time ...staring at falling sand

Wish there was more that I could give You
If I could, I'd fly to the sky and give you all its Blue
And I don't care if everyone says that Its impossible
No matter what the obstacle....This love is so unstoppable

Because even if i must walk a thousand Miles
Even If I have to go through one million Trials
i would do anything to see your perfect Smile
Making its way to me.....walking down the Aisle

Gone Forever

What happened to the chills I used to get...every time I heard your Name
To the feelings that erupted...and were always hard to Tame
To the million butterflies in me...that wished tomorrow never Came
To all those seconds filled with bliss....that have now been replaced with Pain

Everything I felt for you...has quickly gone Away
And Just like you ..my dear..everything just disappeared one Day..
"we'll always be together", isn't that what you always used to Say..
You must of worn ice for shoes...cuz you quickly ran Away

Everything goes numb now... If i ever hear your Name.
Only lingering attachments are the sorrow and the Pain.
All those memories we shared seem to be eating at my Brain..
Even till this day...i still wonder if you ever felt the Same

King of the Damned

As of now....I am done with playing Nice
No longer will I ignore this heart of Ice
I'll make sure its fear that's portrayed through both your Eyes
Making you live in terror is the only thing that will Suffice

Acting like I'm nice has been driving me Insane
Listening to people that keep talking about Pain
Making them feel better..pretending I have felt the Same
The personality I've created is nothing but a Feign

My life up to now has been nothing but a Sham
I was born to raise hell..to be the King of the Damned
Yes I am the Lion and you nothing more than a Lamb
I'm no longer hiding..no more denying who I Am

Love

Its hard to explain everything that I'm feeling Inside
And even without the right words to say..this smile leaves me with nothing to Hide
So lets see if I can find just the right things to Say
To give form to the feelings you make me live with each Day

Every time we talk..you make everything start to feel Right
And these million butterflies in me...seem to start taking Flight
So I can't help but smile and say that I love You
And to love the chills that I get when you say, "I love you Too"

And every time that you talk..your voice takes my breath Away
Thats why I sit in silence..and listen to every word that you Say
I'd never heard it so perfect...the sound of my Name
Babe you're driving me crazy...for you I'm Insane

So here I am...screaming that my heart belongs to You
Swearing that I'll love you forever..please believe it...Its true
You've always been on my side and I promise to never take you for Granted
And even though I don't believe in God...I know..you're the one wish, to me, he has Granted

Addicted

I breathe from the wound on my heart...that you have Afflicted..
But no matter how much pain you have caused....to you I'll be forever Addicted
So hurt me more...yeah tie me down to your Chains
But no matter how much I bleed...you'll forever run through my Veins

I want to break free....to try and live without Pain
But If I try and withdraw...memories start to feed at my Brain
You're the drug that I need....that always helps me to Fly
So just say that you love me....while you look in my Eyes

But if you want me to die...just say that you'll Leave
Without you I can't Live....can hardly even Breathe
So walk past the door....and leave me gasping for Air
Yeah go quench your lust....While you have that Affair

Is it Love?

There is an aching pain that crescendos in my Heart
How can friends and family try and push us to fall Apart
How can they stand there and say our love ain't Real
How the fuck can they tell..when they can't sense how we Feel

But I can see it in your eyes...they inflicted you with Doubt
I can sense you moving farther ...I can feel us falling Out
I can hear it in your voice..how you try and hide your Pain
I know their venomous words...have already infected your Brain

If you want to know if we belong together, the answer is easy to Find
Think back to all the memories we shared..that you've pushed to the back of your Mind
There you will find that what we have can be nothing but Love
A gift that we got...that was God Sent from Above

When it Rains

I'm staring out my window..seeing the falling Rain
And every fallen drop seems.... to be screaming out your Name
A name that brought me warmness ...and overwhelming Pain
I guess with love comes sorrow.. as they're one and the Same

The sky seems to be acting.. exactly like my Eyes
The precipitation comes with ...the reminder of your Lies
And every time a drop falls.. my heart slowly seems to Die
Oh how I hate these stupid eyes..that like to imitate the Sky

Did it ever cross your mind..that it could possibly be Me
That you and I were prefect..and we were really meant to Be
Floating like a butterfly...and stinging like a Bee
Despite how much it hurts...you're the only one for Me

Better than the Truth

So you're getting ready to go out tonight Again
I know where you're headed, and to let you go I must be Insane
To quench your lust..I know you'll be seeing him Tonight
Hiding my tears...I try and stay out of the Light

I always turn a blind eye, and pretend that I don't Know
I always hide in darkness, and watch you as you Go
An idiot for allowing you to do what you Do
But I'll keep on pretending if I never have to lose You

So give me an excuse, hide behind more Lies
Make me feel loved as you look me in the Eyes
Remind me of the good old days we spend throughout our Youth
And I'll keep convincing my heart...sometimes it better to ignore the Truth

If I'm able to be with you each Day
Then I'll believe anything you have to Say
So I'll be hiding all my Pain
So tomorrow we can go back to acting a Feign

Thoughts of Nobody

For too long I have kept my true self hidden Inside
Now even from myself my true self seems to Hide
Even I don't know who is the real Me
Hiding behind masks and facades is who I came to Be

When I look in the mirror ...I don't recognize who I See
Is that who I am...or are other people being projected through Me
Am I truly alive...or just existing through Lies
Even the man in the mirror doesn't seem to have life in those Eyes

I need to know who I am...can't continue living on like This
I don't care what they say...ignorance doesn't feel like Bliss
My life has no meaning...My existing feels Shallow
I'm nothing but a body...an empty vessel that's Hollow

Sun and the Rain

She always tell me that she hates the Rain
That it makes her feel alone, makes her drown in all her Pain
And it seems she can't wait to see the shinning Sun
But unfortunately she feels the rain can't be Outrun

But...I have really come to love the Rain

Washes all my worries and helps keeping me Sane
And its actually the sun that I have come to Hate
As it dries all of the rain, my life it begins to Complicate

So she hates the rain she can't outrun
And I hate my rain being dried by Sun
But if she loves the thing I've come to Hate
How can our meeting ..seem to feel like Fate

But then things became so clear to Me
Suddenly the answer was so easy to See
Why so easily we fell in Love
And there was no rain or sun we were in need Of

She became my rain, washing everything Away
All my fears and worries, she made them disappear one Day
And so she calls me her Sun, always shinning Bright
That always keeps her warm and illuminates her Night

Sleepless Nights

Fallen victim to yet another sleepless Night.
Only my phone's screen shinning Bright
A photo of you being displayed on the Screen
And glistening tears..on my cheek can be Seen

So I relive our story by rereading old Texts
Never thought you would leave me in this world to live in the Next
Wasting your time on me came with a Price
A life time with me, to you, would never Suffice

So I just sit here and Cry
Unable to tell you Goodbye
You were just taken Away
Shadowing my world in shades of Gray

So another night I'll spend alone in this Bed
Just having you, forever, live in my Head
To always be there haunting my Thoughts
To make my heart skip a beat or tie it in Knots

Come Back

Another night I'll spend Alone
Holding on to things you used to Own
I'll lay here and cry myself to Sleep
Hoping you'll appear and wipe the tears off of my Cheek

And everyday I'll pray for it to Rain
For the sky to open up..so you can come down to me Again
So I can once again ..see your shinning Smile
To warm me up inside....even if just for Awhile

All Day I wait for you to walk through the Door
To come and pick my dreams up from the Floor
So please come back and make everything Right
I'll be waiting all day and all Night

You my addiction

There comes a time, in every person's life
When they can't help but truly feel alive
And that's how I feel each and every day
That your perfect smile takes my breath away

You make all my senses feel like they're contradicting
In a way that makes everything feel so addicting
its so hard to control my breathing
When this heart can't seem to stop the beating

Your warm eyes always give me the shivers
My heart nearly stops from the blow your wet kiss delivers
The slightest of touch ..make chills run up and down my spine
Like Im frozen in time....from your look, so Divine

I don't want our relationship to be Lopped
But a few things really will need to be stopped
Love, you have really become my addiction
But for the sake of my life..we're ganna need to have some restrictions

Say that it's worth it

Are you happy where you are....is there no better place for you to Fit....
Tell me that your life is really perfect....that giving up on us was worth It ..
Say that he is worth giving up everything we Had..
From every kiss that we shared to just walking holding Hands

Tell me that he gives you lots of pretty things...worth more than everything I Have
That he is a perfect man..and was worth breaking me in Half
Say that I am nothing and, to him, I could never measure Up
That he is like a grown up dog..I'm nothing but a Pup

You say I have the right to be upset..that you would Understand
But you dont even know...that my legs no longer have the strength to Stand
Ever since you left..everything about me ,surely, Died
I knew you wouldn't be back no matter how many times I Cried

But...I hope he is everything you wished for..and a Spark in you he Lit
That you two can last forever...and you never have to Split
And you dont have to worry at all..of what will become of Me
I'll always keep on living...even if miserable is the best that I can Be

The Mind of Nobody

Having many talents and still not knowing who is the real Me
From the second I was born I was pushed to be the best that I could Be
Born to a strict father that just wouldn't accept Mediocrity
Everyday I honed my skills to become the man you can now See

But my father was in love with trouble and is now rotting behind a Cell
So I jumped off the road he paved for me so I wouldn't end up dying in there as Well
But being my father's son..My true self I began to Hide
Fearing I'd end up like him, I kept my true self bottled up Inside

Loosing sight of who I was, I kept questioning who was the real Me
Evidence pointed to my father....but I just had to Disagree
He has been gone most of my life, so no real input in who I really Am
Even if it runs through my blood, I don't want to have the throne to the Damned

So everyday I pick this pen, to try and unravel my mind that's tide in Knots
Hoping to find my true self who is hiding behind these Thoughts

But my mind is just a haystack and the needle is too hard to See
But I'll keep looking till the end, until I find the one true Me

Regrets in Time

Can you feel as time..is slipping through your Hands
With an hourglass that's broken...impossible to regain the fallen Sand
And every minute passes...leaving hours far Behind
So look through the Kaleidoscope of broken glass...and painful memories you'll Find

Alone you count down to the Death of an Era
And memories leave trails in the form of bleeding Mascara
Time to regret the decisions that'll lead to you dying Alone
No one to stand and cry on the sod....while they look down on your Stone

So go grab the alcohol and a handful of Pills
Time to choke on the objects that for years brought you Thrills
Just lay in your bed and take a long last look at the Sun
For death is knocking at your door and it can't be Outrun

The point of Trying

Tell me now...whats the point of me even Trying
While you're out there having fun.....Im here slowly Dying
Everyday growing colder...as we're moving farther Apart
And it feels Like I've lost...my rightful place in your Heart

And please stop saying that you feel the Same
Look at that smile in your face...and here I am being driven Insane
Everyday I wait..just to speak to you for a Minute..
And when we finally talk...feels like your heart's just not in It

I love you yes...and we both know that its True
But can you please tell me what am I supposed to Do
How can I go on like this....its Torturous
But its like you don't give a fuck...so I don't know what's the point of This

Deadly Collisions

Like a movie, My life seems to be flashing through my Eyes
From the moment I was born, to this moment where I Die
Only the gushing of blood seems to be blurring that Vision
As my body lays broken...from the deadly Collision

My heartbeat is fading..I can feel that I'm Dying
As my world turns to black..It all becomes so Terrifying
The gold of my skin..seems to be fading to Pale
All the medics have struggled...only to Fail

Everything is silent..as I give the last of my Breaths
My thoughts seem to wonder...what will happen after my Death
Will I be going to heaven and be welcomed by God
Or become another corpse that is rotting six feet under the Sod

I am rushed to the hospital so they can try and keep me Alive
But the hope had all died way before I even Arrived
There was nothing to do..nothing more to be Done
Just another life that had ended...before it had Begun

As Everything Ends

There are a few things in life that we just can't Comprehend
Like how everything that starts must come to its End
So tell me now why I was never allowed to say Never
When you always stood there and lied saying you'd love me Forever

It started so beautiful and has now ended in Pain
Leaving me mentally wounded with no strength to Sustain
Memories flourish reminding me of when I first Confessed
But these memories come with this aching pain in my Chest

But with these last few word comes my final Request
No matter what comes your way..I want you to give it your Best
But..Honestly now..I sort of feel Relieved
Without me in your life...you can now accomplish your Dreams

So this is the end...this is our final Goodbye
I just need to wait for tonight..when I can finally Cry

There's nothing more...that to you I must Say
Just try to live happily..as you go on your Way

Unwavering

Do you still remember that first day that we Met
Or when we said Goodbye in the rain soaking Wet
You never made it quite clear what it was you were Feeling
And I could never quite unravel the feelings in your Eyes I was Seeing

But you always knew I was completely in love with You
Always looking to see..if maybe you felt the way I do
Knowing this love would haunt me Forever
Its the only thing my heart can ever Endeavor

Everyday...being completely Infatuated
Unrequited love... making things more Complicated
Bending to your will...I was completely wrapped around your Finger
I always thought..these feelings would be here to haunt and Linger

But then they just vanished without leaving a Trace
And for the first time in ages there was an actual smile on my Face
And who would of thought I would gain happiness from Another
Capturing my heart...and making it admit that it loves Her

She easily makes these feelings for you..seem like they're Nothing
Might be hard to believe...you must think that I'm Bluffing
She has taken over my life..and has now become my Everything
And unlike my feelings for you....my love for her...is forever Unwavering

When Nothing Else matters

Can you tell me what I am meant to feel
If my heart is numb..then why does this pain inside seem so real
Tell me...What the fuck's the Deal..
Isn't this heart made of stone...isn't it unfathomable to think the layers have begun to Peel

But right now I feel so Brittle
Why did it hurt so much...when you said to you I meant so Little
My chest feels hollow....my heart has been Riddled

If to me you mean nothing....how can you make me feel Belittled

It started off as just another one of my Games
To make you fall in love...then leave you drowning in Pain
But it seems as now...You run through my Veins
Could it be than I'm....the one who's been Tamed

Young Blood spilled

Have you ever cut yourself..just to see the blood run Through
Ever kept trying to hurt yourself..thinking no one ever felt like You
And thought that no one will even notice when you Die
Do you hold that blade against you're wrist all night...while tears blind your Eyes

Tell me..have you grown to believe that you'll always be on your Own
Everyday you hide in darkness..cuz you believe you're dying all Alone
And you always act cold..and pretend you left all the painful memories Behind
When in reality they linger there..and feed off of your Mind

Well..you're not alone..many people know exactly how you Feel
And even though its hard to believe,every wound, with time..does Heal
Yes..I know right now the nightmares seem so Real
But soon...the layers of that heart of steal...will soon begin to Peel

So..just keep moving forward with every coming Day
And Even though I'm an Atheist...I say..it Never hurts to Pray
Just keep in mind..that one day everything will get Better
So keep moving forward and keep yourself Together

Let's make it a Challenge

I must admit....I never dreamed I could one day be Admired
To hear "Man, I love your art" are words of which I will never get Tired
But it wasn't easy and a lot of things from me were Required
Putting my all into pieces that my life has Inspired

But don't get me wrong...I'm not here to Boast
I actually think that I suck...and ways to Improve is what I think of Most
But I see a lot of people who's writing can't even compare to what I can Compose
Yet they're the ones who show off...I guess that's just how everything Goes

They always think they're the shit..and try to put people Down
Just cuz they have a little more talent....or are just more Renown
And all I can do is read all those comments..and sit here with a Frown
But its time for me to step up, put them down...and claim that this is my Crown

Waking up to You

I woke up today..and I felt the warmth of your body
And the breathes you exhaled where all landing on me
And the weight of your body...as you laid on my chest
I've had good mornings....but I'll confess... today was the best

All night while we slept...I held you in my arms
I was telling myself..I was protecting you from everything that harms
But it was an excuse ...I just wanted you Near
While you slept ..whisper in your ear....that you're what my heart holds most dear

And its only been a few months...and I can't picture my life without you
In such a short time..we both grew so much because of all we've been through
You gave my life purpose...and soon became more important than water
This is just a poem to tell you that I love you...my beautiful daughter

Cold and Cruel

Manipulating people's hearts...you play with their Emotions
You go behind their back..and laugh at their Devotion
Before breaking their hearts you feed them you're love Potion
The Tears that you have shed could overflow the Oceans

But I know you feel alone..as you crawl into your Bed
You're keeping a facade..while inside you die for Them
And you can try and hide it..but she's always ruining through your head
You try and force a smile but tears are coming out Instead

So keep playing the tough guy..yeah try and play it Cool
While inside you die for her..and how she played you for a Fool
Keep on giving that fake smile...people say's your strongest Tool
I guess we all learn the hard way...the world's just cold and Cruel

The friends that are lost

Have you ever lost someone you never wanted to Lose
It's like life gave you two options and you didn't know which one to Choose
One path gives you happiness at the cost of your Friend
While the other one gives them happiness and you never see them Again

Its like breaking their heart for now...only way to be sure of their Happiness
Yeah life isn't fair...just a huge fucking Mess
In the End..they might hate you...but you know that its Worth it
They'll be happy and you miserable...and to you that's just Perfect

We can't always choose who we want there next to our Side
With all these bumps on the road we don't know who'll stay for the Ride
That's why we treasure everyone who has stayed...and appreciate the ones that we Lost
Keep that special place in our hearts and give Thanks that our paths they have Crossed

To be Awake

Do you know the point of living life...if it'll be spent in Solitude
Where you're labeled as a freak...because you're just Misunderstood
And you're looking up to Lies....just trying to find some Hope
But even god doesn't seem to give to you.....the strength you need to Cope

Because life's a fucking bitch...and nothing's really Fair
And with every shattered dream..comes the tearing out of Hair
And if Living is to Dream...and to Die is to wake Up
Then I'll end this fucking nightmare the next time I try to Cut

So let the floor be my canvas....as I paint a portrait with my Blood
As the world dies in silence....every drop will make a deafening Thud
And soon i will get rid of the hurt.....and the Ache
Because its time...for me...from this..dream..to Awake

Everything we Need

Throughout the whole world...I wish it was only you and I that Exist
I'd live...surviving on that smile of yours....I never learned to Resist

And it would be from your lips..from which everyday I'd Feed
Stealing the breath from your lips...is the only thing my body will Need

Never again will we need to be sheltered from a Storm
You know I'd keep you safe...while you'd keep me Warm
Because babe....all I need...is you right there..by my Side
We don't need the world's approval...we have nothing to Hide

So please take my hand...and we'll pretend no one else in the world is Alive
And to the people who say we wont make it...we'll take their comments..as a Lie
Cuz babe you have me..I have you...And that's all we'll ever need to Succeed
And we'll prove to the world...no matter what, we'll be exactly what the other one Needs

The difference between........

Everything I've ever wanted..has always been juts out of Reach
Like a girl who'll leave me breathless...and incapable of Speech
But... certain circumstances make it impossible to Have
And this miserable empty heart...keeps on being broken up in Half

So I push everyone away....Wont let anyone come near Me
All these tears that I have shed....disappear before anyone can See
Because everyday its harder to believe in happy Endings
When love amounts to nothing... but lying and Pretending

So what good is false love....when you lose everything you begin to Cherish
When a lie destroys your world.....and happiness begins to Perish
But its hard to realize.....that your world has been filled up with Lies
But the moment that you learn the truth....your whole world comes to its Demise

Insane

I think you infected my Brain....its Insane
All the Pain...that has been attached to my Name
Just its Fame...makes tears fall down like the Rain
And its hard to Sustain...all the evil that runs through these Veins

Can this be who I have Become....I am Scum
When did it turn to into Fun.....to see tears, down your cheek, begin to Run

But I'm Done....all these demons that I need to Outrun
I'm evil..yeah..second to None...but I'm through..being the devil's number one Son

Diseased

I wonder what people would do..if I said that I was Dying
Would they come to me crying...or just think that I was Lying
But..its too much to hold alone..and I no longer feel like Trying
And keeping this facade is no longer Satisfying

And as I slowly die...its almost time to say Goodbye
Tears flood my eyes...impossible to keep them Dry
But it hurts more..knowing I'll spend my final days Alone
Wishing someone would have known..it was time to repay the life that God had Loaned

But this is it..I have a disease..Every breath is a Wheeze
Blood spills when I sneeze ...someone give my life some Ease...
I'm begging you..please....just say you wont Leave
Be the strength that I need...to get back up on these Knees

But..its futile I know..because I'm still going to Die
In the end I will cry....but I'll wipe the tears off my Eyes
Might be impossible to smile...but till the end I will Try
Because I want to seem happy...When I say my Goodbyes

The one that Got Away

Everyday I live..with this heart that I Betray
And with no emotions to display...Inside I've begun to Decay
And I'm left with no words..to even begin to Convey
How much I regret..letting you be the one that got Away

And just imagining you..being happy with somebody Else
My blood begins to melt..while my heart Swells
And jealousy attacks every one of my Cells
And its torture....like I'm stuck going through..one million Hells

I just miss you...I need you..next to my Side
I'm sorry I lied..should have swallowed my Pride
And I know that inside...all trust for me Died

And it became the cause..that a future by my side was Denied

And then I got on a unicorn and Flew over the Rainbow >_<

She loves me....She loves me Not

There goes another rose...telling me "She loves me Not"
As Gravity grabs hold..and in my chest..ties my hopes into a Knot
But I move on to the next rose...and pretend the last outcome I Forgot
Hoping a rose out there will say you love me...cuz babe hope is all I've Got

But you never look my way..and even hope is starting to go Astray
And it feels like asking it to stay..is like my own heart I Betray
Because it hurts everyday...and It feels like i'm starting to Decay
I'm falling apart..but I'll hold on...because deep down I know..I'll have you Someday

But you don't understand..how much i struggle to Stand
Your indifference has wounded my heart...like these thorns have my Hand
And its hard to hold on..and I can't do it for Long
Tell me what I must do to show you...That we are meant to Belong

The end of a Year

I can't believe time..has flown by..and its already been a Year.
And I know that we've both shed some tears...but mostly we smiled from ear to Ear
Yeah...I know that I can"t say our relationship is perfect....Even though to me it Is
We've had fighting and crying..but always turned them into moments of Bliss

It was only a year down...and it was meant to be a life time to Go
But as this relationship ran its course...A gap began to Grow
I guess you reap what you sow...and its time for us to Let Go
And a future by each other's side is another thing we'll never get to Know

And it kills me to know..I'll never be by your Side
But I've come to realize...being with you..will always be Denied
But..I want you to be happy..Like you were always meant to Be
And I hope you find..with who you belong...And we both know that's not Me

Love: 2

How can a smile make all these feeling Erupt
And the glow of your eyes...warm this cold heart I Corrupt
How can it be..that I miss you...If I never had you Before
And how can every time that we talk... only makes me want you even More

How can it be..that you have my heart so Captivated
Like all my hopes elevated and from my fears I've become Liberated
And its been there for a while...i noticed...and trying to stop was Futile
I really can't seem to get rid of this Smile

I was lost within myself ..I had lost all sight of the Light
And I was just walking towards death...because unconsciously..my own death I Invite
But ever since I met you...I began to treasure every Moment
Getting caught up in this bliss..and enjoying every night like we Own It

This is crazy..so crazy..its really Insane
Been through hurt...through .pain....and goodbyes in the Rain
Hard to let go of the bonds and the chains...and to forget all the Names
But I feel like tonight I can smile again....so don't let my feelings for you be in Vain

Run to the Light

So long ago..I gave up my Right to the Light
Sacrificed my heart to the darkness..and it still holds it Tight
And I became a creature that lurks and hunts through the Night
Your neck I will bite....and it'll be the death of you..when I seduce you Tonight

This smile and these eyes...Anyone would think they're Divine
With the perfect complexion and a strong Jaw Line
And you'll get chills from my touch..as my fingers I run down your Spine
You'll be begging for more..As I'm making you Mine

But its really all just an act...and you should run for your Life
Because my heart's turned to ice..And my fangs will slice your neck like a Knife
So you should run towards the light....if you want to Survive
Because if of you I grab hold...you won't be going home back Alive

Your biggest Mistake

You say I'm the reason behind your Heart Ache.. you call me your biggest Mistake
The reason you're laying awake..with memories you can't seem to Shake
Of this love that we faked...I was the only heart you couldn't Break
And your heart I forsake and its too much for you to Take

But we're the same....and You knew that from the Start
You can try and play it smart...But we've turned breaking hearts into an Art
And its insane...As we lure them in the Dark
We shoot them one of cupid's darts....and captivate their Hearts

But you thought you would win...you approached me with a devilish Grin
And I accepted your challenge...and my smile gave you the cue to Begin
And you tried to seduce me with your skin...unleashing the monster Within
We were both having fun...so addicted to Sin

But did you think...that with my heart it would be easy to play..That I'd ask you to Stay
That I'd cry in the shade..because my heart you Betray
Well I hope you regret ..walking my way..Cuz my heart's made of Clay
That I filled your life with Dismay..and hope that you learned I can easily just walk Away

Drowning in the Dark

Long ago..in the middle of the night...on a night exactly like Tonight
When childish dreams still held me Tight
When this life couldn't seem more Bright
I lost sight of the Light....and till this day you haven't made it Right

But how can it be right...when we never got to say Goodbye
In a night you were never meant to die...Six years and we're still begging its a Lie
Hard to believe what we saw before our eyes...there laid a body that we couldn't Recognize
From a heart that warmed our lives ..only remained a body cold as Ice

I'm living in the past..Surviving basking in the Sadness
Letting these memories roam free...even though they're not Harmless
And we're all still drowning in the Dark..with these memories tearing us Apart
As fear ruins our lives...and the Darkness overwhelms our Hearts

Hard to say Goodbye

Its hard to say goodbye...even if we've said goodbye so many times Before
This time a part of me will die...cuz you know you're someone I Adore
And I can't take it anymore..You're not meant to leave again..you Swore
Of course I'm sad...but want to wish you nothing but the best...so these emotions are at War

And you should know...I still remember the first time we said Hello
Was so long ago....funny how the time has Flown
And like us...the memories have Grown...and they're something that I'll never Throw
Tonight you make me say goodbye.....when I really don't want to let you Go

And I'm not going to Lie....the conflicting of emotions..can make it easy for me to Cry
And I wont deny....feels like a huge part of our history will Die
But I'm hoping time will fly....and soon enough, again, we'll be saying "Hi"
But until you decide to come back....this will have to be our Goodbye

Seeking Solace

I linger in this darkness..pretending to be Brave
Wishing something could save..and free me from these emotions that Enslave
And yes I'm a dead man...because to you, my Life, I Gave
But I still wonder through this darkness..cuz I'm scared to be alone laying in that Grave

But I am dead....and we both know you are to Blame
Ever since you came..I have never been the Same
Look what I became.....so fragile I break...every time I hear your Name
Did you plan to leave me like this all along....tell me...was this always your Aim

I'm begging you please..someone give this heart some Comfort
Someone save me form this grave..before my coffin is buried in Dirt
Because with effort...I know...from this path to death I can Divert
But I need someone to trick this heart and make it feel Unhurt

Falling from Grace

Negativity..enslaves me to live this life so Fearfully
Its the only way that I can be.....enjoying dread so Cheerfully
Don't you agree...With all the death I've come to See
There's no surprise that this is Me

And it wasn't hard to predict..of course I am Sick
I've been treated like shit..and been classified as a Spic
So bring out all of the sticks..and if I'm down you should Kick
But you wont bruise me you dicks..because my skin is too Thick

And I'm acquainted with death..it always stares at my Face
So I keep it close in to heart...as it hold me in its tight Embrace
Cuz my life is a waste..and I'm a Disgrace
Maybe I was an angel once...but I've fallen from Grace

Missing Rain

I was your sun..you were my rain..but now you're gone..and this drought is driving me Insane
Without you there's only pain...Memories are a virus to my Brain
I need you back...to keep me sane...please tell me you want the Same
Because..every time I hear your name....I hear thunder...but see no Rain

And you've been gone for awhile...but I'm still living in Denial
That my heart can be this fragile...and its impossible to Smile
All Day I just want to give up and dial...but I know that its Futile
Because I know that you hate me..and my existence is Vile

Sometimes I wish I could Forget..to live a life of No Regret
I'll be a sun with a sunset...and memories of you will turn to Silhouette
No reason to be Upset...to owe my life..to have this Debt
But even if life...had a reset.......I'd never give away the day we Met

Break Away

I want to break away...I want to be Free
Once again I'd like to see...what its like to be Me
To not give it a thought...and do exactly what I Want
To be free from these emotions...that always seem to Haunt

But how can I free myself..when my own heart I Betray
When these emotions always sway..and I kill myself with every passing Day
But my heart is my prison..and these emotions are what keep me Imprisoned
I long for that freedom that I've always Envisioned

But its time to leave it all behind..to start this life Anew
To break away from these emotions...and every thought of You
And its time for me..to make this life my Own
To finally be free...Even if I'll always be Alone

Heaven

My face gets red like I'm sick with a Fever
I want to believe every time that I see Her
That happiness exists, and that she is where I'll find my moments of Bliss
There are things I've never had that I miss..Like her warmth and her Kiss

But yes, Heaven does exist..For I've found it in Her
Though my life is a blur..She helps me Endure
Abandoned by Love, left to starve as a Waif
Then I see her smile and this heart, once again, can feel Safe

But if she is Heaven then I must be Hell
Begging to be saved from the pain where I Dwell
Here I was drowning alone in the Dark
But then she appeared an lit all these Emotions in my Heart

I may not believe in God..but I know that Heaven is Real
I know because of these emotions for her that I Feel
She is the only one that can still make me believe in Love
And it does feel like a gift...that was God sent from Above

Blue and Black

Can you tell me what went wrong
If we're not meant to belong...were you playing with my heart all along
How did it end up like this...you became so remiss
And it seems that now the only time I find peace..is when I think back and reminisce

But how can I move on..when you're everything I miss
When I'm still living off the breaths...stolen from your kiss
When everything I do...revolves around my every thought of you
Imprisoned by a painful past...that we just can't Undo

And I wish I could start anew...

But as time flew..these feelings only Grew
If only we could get on track...and your feelings for me would come back
Then I wouldn't be dying like this..and this heart wouldn't be so blue and black

Innocence

Everything around me is messed up...isn't making much sense
Have these eyes become clouded since I lost innocence
Because looking through them..things no longer seem blessed
It might be the stress..but everything feels like a mess

My dreams...have evolved into devilish Schemes
And they seems...to be fueled... by my heart's painful screams
And this mask that I wear ..helps to keep my true self hidden inside
But with loss of innocence..even that might have died

What happened to the kid that was so clean and Pure
Did his heart become obscure ...as he grew more mature
But the darkness draws in..as it becomes more allure
We all need a cure....to keep innocence secure

Still to be Found

Will I be able to tell..the second that we meet
Will I tell by the way that you'll make my heart beat
Or will it be your smile that will give it away
How will I tell..you're the girl for whom I wait..every day

Will I be head over heals..when I find out you're Real
My heart you will steal..and will I know immediately it's you..by the way I feel
There should be no mistake, it wont be too late
I know when I find you..that you'll be worth the wait

I look up at these stars...and I wonder where you are
And I want to believe it in my gut, that you're really not far
But I've looked everywhere and you're just nowhere to be found
and I just want to believe you'll be there one day when I turn around

But its hard to keep hoping that one day you'll be there
When I've looked everywhere..and couldn't find you anywhere

And I'm growing afraid....and need you to come to my aid
Because doubt will take over...and my heart it will completely invade

Where are you my dear..I hope that you're near
Won't you please appear and get rid of this fear
But I wont be losing hope ..I'll be waiting for years
So if you ever come to find me..you know I'll be here

My last Valentine

I know that I'm...just wasting my time.
no matter how hard i try...he'll always be on your mind
And tonight..you were meant to be my Valentine.
but you're moving closer to him...and leaving me far behind.

And I swear.....even if he'll always be there
you'll be here in my heart...I don't care If I can't compare
If to you I just wont be there.....Yeah I'll always think its unfair...
Babe loving you is a dream that feels more like a nightmare

Tonight....would you be my last Valentine
Just ..once..let me hold you and pretend like you're mine
Feel everything's right..and for us the stars will align
But tomorrow I'll give up..and from this love business I will Resign

Abused

How many people have to go...that I never want to Lose
How many more hits can I take..before my heart's completely Bruised
Its either being alone or being hurt..and from the two I just can't Choose
But when both amount to being the same...it leaves my heart Confused

And my heart's been misused....its been totally abused
And everyday it gains more scars...and wears them as tattoos
Yeah..no wonder its confused...If Cupid did exist..he'd be amused
Don't tell me those three words again..they've become taboo

Maybe I gave this heart...so easily to you
I had given up on love..but somehow my hope you had renewed
But this couldn't last forever...somehow I always Knew
You always thought of him...so I knew this heartache was all that could ensue

My last angel

I'll confess...I'm not Strong
I breakdown every time I hear our song.
And I know that I was wrong
I couldn't prove to them that we Belong

Yeah..I'll confess
That I fucked up...I'm a Mess
There's no words that could help me express
That this heart's filled with distress

But what can I do..If I no longer have you
Even if I beg to your god..the past isn't something that I can Undo
And I wish, from the start...that I knew
That I was a sky....that was loosing its blue

Who would have known that I'd be so empty.
that there was so many things that could easily tempt me
think back to what was wrong with us..I'm sure you'll think of Plenty
I don't believe in god...but I know you're the last angel that he'll send me

We're all Alone

Why is it so hard To Believe
That there's nobody out There
Whether we Cry, Die, or Live
Nobody Really Cares

We are all just Afraid
To be here Alone
Nobody to come to our Aid
We'll always be on our Own

No matter how much we Cry
And try to believe in our Mind
We can search all the Sky
But there's nothing out there to Find

Lost at Sea

Why do I....hear your voice in every song.
Every lyric lies...and tells me that we Belong
But the songs don't notice that you're gone
Or notice this depression that I'm on

Its like... subliminally..every song talks to Me
And in them all I see....is how we're meant to be
Yeah...I know you don't agree...
but let me prove to you....this love wasn't lost at sea

So don't tell me that its dead....that it only lives inside my head
With every tear that we have shed..saying you rather be alone instead
this path that we have led....without you ..its only dread
Listen to the words that I have said.....don't leave me alone in this huge Bed

Ascend

Just like everyone.... I Sin
There's a monster here that sleeps within
And it wants to break out of my skin
Lots of demons that I have to fight....and I can't seem to win

And I guess..I'm a mess
Everyday I care less
Am I fucked? I'd say "Yes"
HA! there's no curse that feels like you're blessed

But I have paid the price for my mistakes
I'm freshly wounded..this heart aches
And everyday it continues to still break
Every morning I awake...with dreadful nightmares I can't shake

And I hurt....I've been dragged through mud and dirt
This heart's slowly starting to convert
My personality is starting to invert
Turning to a demon is something I just can't seem to divert

This is it...this is the end
My own broken heart I have to Mend

I'm a perfect blend...of demon and godsend
And I have come to realize..that my sinning will help me to Ascend

Irreplaceable

Why can't I..seem to forget about you
In every girl..all I seem to spot..are the things that resemble you
And its driving me Mad...thinking about everything that we had..
yeah I'm living in the past..don't care if everyone says that its bad

I'm going deaf...these ears block out all of the noise
And I don't have a choice...they only wish for the sound of your voice
I want it....but you don't make a sound
I need you...why are you nowhere to be found

Baby..please...you just need to come back
No matter how many girls I have found....they all have things that they lack
None of them have what it takes to be you
So...please come back..there are many things we need to undo

The Perfect Imperfection

Lets speak the truth...what we had was never perfect
We would always fight..yet the seconds of bliss would make it seem worth it
And I know I made you sad..I kept driving you mad
But think back to what we had.........was it really too bad

Yes we would fight..we'd break up every night
But every morning we'd make up..and again things would start to feel right
Things started to get rough...they were becoming too tough
Then one day you decided that you'd finally had enough

But no matter how much you hate it..I'll always be your first
You had such a lustful heart..and only I could quench its Thirst
So go ahead and hate me..and say that you don't love me
But every time you see the word "love" you will always think of me

And this is what we were...just a perfect imperfection
Hate it all you want..but you just can't go denying our connection
And this love's become rejected..and our hearts become neglected
But babe..no matter what we do...we'll never be completely disconnected

In the eyes of God

I'm staring at my phone...just waiting for your call
Thinking of how you would make this heart fly...as you slowly made it fall
But right now I don't even think that it can crawl
Because you were taken from me,....and this heart can't beat if you're not here at all

But this relationship..was forbidden from the start
And I knew that I would fall apart...if I let you in my heart
Now I'm drowning in the dark...as slowly you depart
And Maybe we were sinning..but it was as beautiful as art

Well I don't care if what we had is considered sin
Love becomes adrenaline and makes our whole head spin
Laughs and stupid grins...with Goosebumps on the skin
How can it be evil..if happiness is bursting from within

Well maybe it is wrong..looking through the eyes of God
You're now another perfect lady....who now believes she's Flawed
Don't silently agree....Don't just give up and Nod
You can go now and pretend to live happily ..but we'll both know you're keeping a façade

Gospel of Love

Let me say this from the start...I wasn't sent from HELL
I was just another normal boy..who created SIN when for you I FELL
I didn't mean to test your FAITH..or prevent you from getting SAVED
Simply wanted to show you how fun it was to Misbehave

I started off on my own..wondering these seven days alone
But when you appeared the first signs of life, from me, where shown
Then the apples came to tempt me...these were the first test that life had sent me
And when I took that bite...for the first time I felt completely empty

Well now comes forth our Apocalypse
We're done and now I die when I imagine someone else feeding off your lips
Slowly starting to descend....everyday its harder to force a smile and pretend
Maybe Its just a heartbreak but it feels like my whole world is coming to an End

Estoy Enamorado de Ti

No point in pretending we both know I'm in love with you
But everyday this heart dies because of all you put me through
No I'm not trying to complain...though I do live with constant pain
But every day this love dies because I know that to your heart I do the same

Remember all I wrote down when I sent you that letter
Don't think I stubbornly live in the past without wanting to forget her
Because I do...I just want to throw her memory Away
But when I'm so close to doing it..something tells me that she's here to stay

And I'm losing you I know...and its not her Its Me
How I dragged you along ..by my side selfishly
But don't think you're the only one..who stays up all night and Cries
Because this heart dies..and at night..its impossible to dry the tears from my eyes

Thank You

All My life I've had things that I thought I didn't deserve
And although this is the same...this is something that I want to preserve
And What I've got now...Is all these people that tell me I can and push me to be a better Man
And although I don't deserve you ..I'm thankful....to everyone that calls themselves my Fan

Thank you....for putting up with me even though I'm completely insane
And when I have writer's block...and every poem keeps sounding the same
And without you..I really..don't know what I'd do
I'd be like a bird who lacked courage and never actually flew

My self-esteem is shattered, by my own negativity its been reduced
But your words always help to give this confidence a boost
I don't mean these words to sound redundant but I just want to say "Thank You"
And know that every time I post another poem Up...its because you helped me through

Tonight

I'm looking at old texts on my Phone
Hoping you're laying on that bed Alone
Wondering if he was with you Tonight
If he was holding you tight

For.. I need you Tonight
Need you to make this Alright
Its been a year since that Fight
I no longer care which one of us was Right

I want you to kiss me Goodnight
For you to hold me real Tight
For you to never let me Go
Whenever you hug me Hello

The Price of Freedom

I always thought I wanted freedom....
But I never though it'd feel like this
Every night just reminiscing
about everything I miss
And I'm still left here..gasping..searching
for that breath you stole from our last kiss
So I'll spend another night here crying
As this lonely heart keeps dying

But no
I don't blame you at all
You didn't force me to fall
You're not there forcing me awake all night
helplessly waiting for a call
That of course i know will never come.
The past is already gone
and no matter how much we wish to change things
we both know what's done is done

So I'll just stay here alone
And let this heart continue to break
I'll be living off the memories...
and continue to fall with every breath I take
And you know that what I'll do
my every breath belongs to you
Yeah I know that you'll move on
but don't you dare forget what we've been through

I wanted to give you freedom....
But I never thought it'd feel like this

But no
I don't blame you at all
You didn't force me to fall
You're not there forcing me awake all night
helplessly waiting for a call
That of course i know will never come.
The past is already gone
and no matter how much we wish to change things
we both know what's done is done

To Juliet

Wake up Juliet..get up from that Bed
Your eyes may still be closed...but I know that you're not dead
Remember..Everything I said
Happy...or tragic..Together we'll be moving towards the End
Forget about the poison...thoughts of drinking it..no longer cross my head

Last Letter to Juliet

Dear Juliet

This is the last time that I write you a letter
I've tried to move on..but there's no signs of things ever getting better
My heart wants you to be happy but at the same time screams out "go and get her"
A bird that lost its feathers.. a prisoner to love..chained by fetters

But there's no moving on when only you can be my Juliet
A dream planted in my head..of a future so vague...I can see in silhouette
I haven't completely let go yet ..but if I do..I'll live with regret
But I'm tired of waking up each morning with these tears leaving my pillows soaking wet

I can't do this anymore...you've taken over my every thought
Memories ..with eyes teary...building in this throat a knot
My heart you caught...and gave it the happiness that it sought
But in the end..love was only a painful lesson to be taught

But this is the End...On this broken hope I can't depend
To this heart I have to tend..find a way to completely Mend
Can no longer act content...this smile is too hard to pretend
Every time I said "I love you" it had a meaning you could never comprehend

My every morning

I wake up and I'm struggling to breathe
And I scream out "don't leave"
Like if you were still standing by me
But I'm just half asleep
And the scene in my head is too painful to see
The day that you left me to be
Just a hollow version of me

And I look at my hands..that still feel the warmth of your skin
And all of this pain starts to burst from within
Its been a few weeks and I wonder how you have been
Then my head starts to violently spin
Always promise not to think of you..yet always give in
Its quite a predicament...this situation we're in
I'll keep trying to hold out..but needing you doesn't allow me to win

So I blink
and the tears start to rain down as black ink
and these thoughts..with the page starts to link
For one moment..all the pain..to this pen starts to sync
And this page..express in rhyme..every emotion that painfully slinks
Because you know that since you left you're in every thought that I think
Without you I'm meeting extinction..feels like I'm already at the Brink

Reason for Broken Wings

He is..someone...who can never pursue his dreams
Always..dreading what the future brings
Looking calm..but inside his heartbeat screams
These are..his reason for broken wings

Inside...he isn't quite how he seems
Never shows....but inside he's ruled by grief
In his heart the darkness reigns supreme
Begs for happiness...even if the moment's brief

Only through writing can he blow some steam
But not once..has he known what its like to feel relief
All his emotions seem to overflowing the brim
Even his heart seems to be becoming stiff

Lost in thoughts of You

I feel so lost again
As days pass by...the grief gets harder to contain
I just want to break down and complain
Its hard to explain..but I just can't sustain
All the pain...that everyday I obtain
Its insane..but I don't want to refrain
Even if it hurts I'll think of you..until nothing of me can remain

You were my poison..and my brain is stuck hearing voices
Your voice...and every time it secretly rejoices
For a moment..everything's pointless...Brain blocks out all of the noises
And everyday I keep wishing we could have made different choices

But the past is gone..and its something we can't Undo
All we can do....is go on our way..and start life anew
Though I can't..since this brain only ever thinks of you
My poison...my glue....that held me together..its true
And I knew.....since the first time you said you loved me too
That no matter what we went through
This heart could only belong to you

The thrill

I always end up putting myself in these kinds of situations
I've long stopped believing in love...but always fall for these temptations
Like a challenge..the thrill.....my heart loves the sensations
But this Lust....this sinning....my soul's in need of salvation

But this heart loves to pray on the heart of the innocent
As slowly they breaks..the thrill so magnificent.
I'm not evil I swear..but the act..feels so reminiscent
Reminds me of her...of the past...her heart so Maleficent

I do what she did..to my heart everyday
Give them hope...make them fall...then just take it away
It hurts but the thrill makes everything worth it.
To relive..everyday..what i went through with her..makes everything perfect

Moving on

I need to stop...to stop being Me
Change who I am...and become the man I need to Be
I need to leave my past..and just throw my worries to the sea
Hope the pain doesn't catch up to me..so I can finally be Free

But before I move on...my.own heart I must Master
Because these demons inside are all full of Laughter
Laughing at me for being a walking Disaster
With no dreams ....and no future.. and no idea of what I'm After

But I must move on...and Just accept that you're Gone
Get back into the world from which myself I've Withdrawn
Throw away that past that this heart keeps dwelling Upon
When the night breaks dawn...I will be a different man...I WILL have moved On

Young Blood Spilled: part 2

You've done it again
Now the blood drips down your hands
You inflict yourself pain
thinking that no one understands

You hide it so well
Because you think no one feels like you
Think you're condemned to hell
And no one knows what you've been through

How could they know
If they've never worn your shoes
Only know what you're willing to show
And don't show how your heart is bruised

You're always wearing a smile
But keep your true feeling bottled up inside
In truth your heart is so fragile
And have so many tears that try so hard to hide

But stop
Don't do it again
Let the blade drop
And stop causing self-pain

The addiction

Helps replace the hurt from your heart
Your Affliction
And it keeps tearing you apart

Stop...you're losing so much blood
Look to your side and we'll help keep you strong
Wipe those tears that your eyes seem to flood
so you can clearly see your friends have been by your side all along

We may not understand
But know that you're not on your own

We'll always be your helping hand
So know the pain's not your burden alone

A Night with Someone Else

Why am I like this
Just lying to myself
I'm feeding off your lips
While I think of someone else

I hold you in my arms
But inside I think of her
The thought of her still harms
Its not one I can endure

I thought with you I could forget
And get her off my mind
But I haven't left her yet
But I'm still trying to make You Mine

Its Driving me Insane
I look at you and I see her
Bite my lip to stop from screaming out her name
And thank the tears..that my vision blur

How will I get through the night
If she will always appear in my vision
I try to concentrate on you..to make it feel right
But it feels like my heart is imprisoned

The night is gone
And you didn't notice a thing
Wish I could feel like I won
but the pain in my heart really Stings

Reminisce about the Past

What do you do ..when you lose someone that was always there for you
That no matter how tough life seemed to get...she always helped you through
But then suddenly decides she's had enough of you..wants to start her life anew
Then leaves you in the dead of night..without a clue of what to do

Sometimes I just lay awake at night..and wonder about your new life
wonder if you're still alive...or if now you're someone's new wife
I took you for granted so it justifies paying up this cruel price
And I've...spent so many nights just crying.. reminiscing about our old life

Well whoever says that men don't cry..must have never heard of pain
Must of never of had someone live inside their brain.Have them running through their veins...
Must have never of known how much it hurts..sometimes..to hear that certain person's name
Men must be dry like the dessert.....but even the Sahara has it's rain

www.ingramcontent.com/pod-product-compliance
Lightning Source LLC
Chambersburg PA
CBHW042123040426
42450CB00002B/50